P9-ELT-130

*S*ince they were introduced more than 85 years ago, Oreo® cookies have delighted generation after generation of cookie lovers—kids and adults alike. That's why Nabisco® is thrilled to bring you *Oreo® with a Twist*, an exciting collection of recipes made with "America's Favorite Cookie." Containing 75 recipes for cakes, pies, cheesecakes, snacks and more, this book will show you how to enjoy Oreo cookies in delicious new ways. And because each recipe has been tested in both the Nabisco Food Center and the *Better Homes and Gardens*® Test Kitchen, you can be assured of successful results every time.

As you page through the book, our mascot—Oreo Man—will guide you on a delectable journey, sharing with you his favorite recipes and pointing out facts, games and cooking tips.

So turn the page and begin the joy of making—and eating—these wonderful Oreo delights.

Pictured on the Cover:
OREO® Cheesecake (recipe, page 9)

This seal assures you that every recipe in *Oreo® with a Twist* has been tested in the *Better Homes and Gardens*® Test Kitchen. This means that each recipe is practical and reliable, and meets high standards of taste appeal.

© Copyright 1998 Nabisco, Inc.
© Copyright 1998 Meredith Corporation.
All Rights Reserved. Printed in the United States of America.
Printing Number and Year: 5 4 3 2   02 01 00 99
Library of Congress Catalog Card Number: 98-68025
ISBN: 0-696-20956-X
Canadian BN 12348 2887 RT.

Produced by Meredith Integrated Marketing,
1716 Locust Street, Des Moines, IA 50309-3023. The
Better Homes and Gardens® Test Kitchen Seal is a registered
trademark of Meredith Corporation.

"Bubble Yum," "Comet," "Fruit Stripe," "Honey Maid," "Knox," "Life Savers," "Oreo," "Planters," "Royal," "Snackwell's," "Teddy Grahams" and "Toastettes" are registered trademarks of Nabisco Brands Company.

"America's Favorite Cookie"

Credits

Editorial and Design
Meredith Integrated Marketing

Recipe Development
Nabisco Food Center
Better Homes and Gardens® Test Kitchen

Nabisco Project Manager
Katrina Sanders Yolen

Photography
King Au; Studio Au, Inc.
Andy Lyons, Cameraworks

Prop Styling
Dana Etzel

Food Styling
Lynn Blanchard
Jennifer Peterson

Illustrations
Jim Swanson

Table of Contents

~

Through the Years

Whether enjoyed with a cold glass of milk or crumbled and used for cooking, Oreo is "America's Favorite Cookie." But just how did this legendary cookie get its start? The story goes as follows: In 1912, the National Biscuit Company (later changing its name to Nabisco Brands, Incorporated) introduced three new biscuits or cookies—Mother Goose, Veronese and Oreo—to meet their customers' demands for English-style biscuits. Although the first two have long since disappeared, the crispy chocolate wafers with a rich creme filling endured to become not only America's favorite cookie, but also the world's best-selling cookie.

In recent years, the folks at Nabisco have continued to create delectable variations on this tasty cookie. Here's a list of when each was developed.

Origin of the Name

There are many tales of how Oreo got its name. But since no written records exist, nobody knows for sure. One theory states that because the cookies originally came in a gold-colored package, Oreo was derived from *or*, the French word for gold. Another story claims that since the first Oreo cookies were hill-shaped, the name came from the Greek word for mountain, *oreo*. Yet another professes that Nabisco used the "re" from the word "creme" and sandwiched it between two "o's" taken either from the word "chocolate" or from the round shape of the cookie. No matter where it came from, Oreo is a word—and cookie—that is understood and loved around the world.

Oreo Introductions

1912—OREO Cookies

1974—OREO DOUBLE STUF Cookies

1987—Fudge Covered OREO Cookies

1990—White Fudge Covered OREO Cookies

1991—Halloween OREO Cookies

1995—Holiday OREO Cookies

1996—50% Reduced Fat OREO Cookies

1997—Spring OREO Cookies

Cookie-Cooking Tips

Making family-pleasing recipes with Oreo® cookies is easy and fun if you know the following dessert-making tricks of the trade.

Crushing Cookies: To **finely crush** Oreo cookies, place them in a large plastic bag and seal it. Then, using a rolling pin, crush the cookies until they are about the size of cornmeal.

Chopping Cookies: When a recipe calls for **finely chopped** Oreo cookies, use a sharp knife to cut them into tiny uniform pieces about the size of peppercorns. For **coarsely chopped** cookies, cut them into small uniform pieces about the size of blueberries.

Splitting Cookies: There are two ways to split Oreo cookies. To keep the filling all on one side of the cookie, use the end of a metal spatula to separate one of the chocolate wafers from the filling. For filling on both wafers, use a sharp knife to carefully cut through the center of the filling.

Halving Cookies: To cut Oreo cookies into semicircles, carefully cut across the cookies with a serrated knife using a gentle sawing motion.

Serving Frozen Desserts: Before serving a frozen dessert, let it stand at room temperature to slightly soften. Allow 5 to 10 minutes for small items and 20 to 30 minutes for larger desserts.

Substituting Oreo Cookies: For recipes in this book, if you like, you can substitute

OREO® Banana Split Pie (recipe, page 31)

Reduced Fat Oreo cookies for regular Oreo cookies. Also, you can substitute the regular cookies in recipes calling for Holiday Oreo cookies, and you can substitute Oreo Double Stuf cookies for Halloween or Spring Oreo cookies. (*Halloween Oreo* cookies are available from the end of September through October, *Holiday Oreo* cookies in mid-November through December and *Spring Oreo* cookies in mid-February through April.)

Finely Crushed

Finely Chopped

Coarsely Chopped

Double
Delicious
Desserts

Scrumptious desserts are sure to satisfy everyone's cravings. Serve these luscious cakes, pies and parfaits—made extra delicious with Oreo® cookies—as a simple sweet ending to a family meal or the crowning touch to a special celebration.

OREO® Mud Pie (recipe, page 8)

OREO® Mud Pie

Prep Time: 20 min. • Freeze Time: 4 hrs. and 10 min.

Customize this tempting mud pie by replacing the coffee ice cream with another flavor. You can even create a patchwork pie by using several different ice creams (photo, page 7).

  26 **OREO Chocolate Sandwich Cookies, divided**
    2 **tablespoons butter *or* margarine, melted**
    1 **pint chocolate ice cream, softened**
    1 **pint coffee ice cream, softened**
  ½ **cup chocolate fudge topping**
  ½ **cup heavy cream, whipped**
  ¼ **cup PLANTERS Walnuts *or* PLANTERS COCKTAIL Peanuts, chopped**

❶ Finely crush 12 cookies; mix crushed cookies and butter in bowl. Press firmly on bottom of 9-inch pie plate. Stand remaining 14 cookies around edge of plate. Freeze 10 minutes.

❷ Carefully spread chocolate ice cream into prepared crust. Scoop coffee ice cream into balls; arrange over chocolate layer. Freeze 4 hours or until firm.

❸ Top pie with fudge topping, whipped cream and walnuts. Makes 7 servings.

How Do You Eat an Oreo Cookie?

BITE

Dunk it? Take big bites, little bites or one giant bite? Nibble the edges first? Twist it open and lick the creme filling? How do you eat an Oreo cookie? Oreo Man says that 50% of all Oreo cookie eaters pull them apart first, with women twisting them open more often than men.

OREO® Cheesecake

Prep Time: 20 min. • Bake Time: 50 min. plus cooling • Chill Time: 4 hrs.

What could be better than the marriage of rich, creamy cheesecake and Oreo cookies? This classic dessert is sure to please all the Oreo fans (photo, front cover)!

1	(1-pound 4-ounce) package **OREO Chocolate Sandwich Cookies, divided**
¼	cup butter *or* margarine, melted
2	(8-ounce) packages cream cheese, softened
¾	cup sugar
3	eggs
1	(16-ounce) container sour cream
1	teaspoon vanilla extract
	Dark sweet cherries *and* mint sprigs, for garnish

❶ Reserve 6 cookies for garnish. Finely crush half the remaining cookies. Coarsely chop remaining half of cookies; set aside.

❷ Mix finely crushed cookies and butter in bowl. Press firmly on bottom and 1½ inches up side of 9-inch springform pan; set aside.

❸ Beat cream cheese and sugar in large bowl with electric mixer at medium speed until creamy. Blend in eggs, sour cream and vanilla; fold in coarsely chopped cookies. Spread mixture into prepared crust.

❹ Bake at 350°F for 50 to 60 minutes or until set. Cool at room temperature for 1 hour. Refrigerate at least 4 hours.

❺ Remove side of pan. Halve reserved cookies. Garnish cheesecake with cookie halves, cherries and mint. Makes 12 servings.

Baked OREO® Custards

Baked OREO® Custards

Prep Time: 20 min. • Bake Time: 50 min. plus cooling

Old-fashioned baked custards take on a whole new attitude when studded with blissful chunks of Oreo cookies. The custards are equally delicious served at room temperature or chilled.

12 **OREO Chocolate Sandwich Cookies, divided**

2 **cups half-and-half *or* light cream**

5 **egg yolks, slightly beaten**

⅓ **cup sugar**

1 **teaspoon vanilla extract**

⅛ **teaspoon salt**

  Thawed frozen whipped topping, for garnish

❶ Halve 3 cookies; reserve 5 halves for garnish. Coarsely chop remaining cookie half and 4 whole cookies.

❷ Heat half-and-half in small saucepan over medium heat just until bubbles form around edge of pan; set aside.

❸ Beat egg yolks, sugar, vanilla and salt in large bowl with electric mixer at medium speed until smooth; slowly beat in hot half-and-half.

❹ Place 5 (6-ounce) custard cups in 13x9x2-inch baking pan. Pour custard mixture evenly into cups. Top each cup with 1 tablespoon chopped cookies and 1 whole cookie. Set pan on center oven rack. Pour enough hot water into baking pan to reach halfway up the sides of cups.

❺ Bake at 325°F for 50 to 55 minutes or until knife inserted near center comes out clean. Remove cups from water and cool on wire rack.

❻ Garnish each custard with whipped topping and halved cookie. Makes 5 servings.

Marbled Cheese Pie With Raspberry Sauce

Prep Time: 15 min. • Bake Time: 35 min. plus cooling • Chill Time: 4 hrs.

For a pretty presentation, drizzle some of the raspberry sauce in a zigzag pattern over individual dessert plates before placing slices of this elegant pie on the plates. Serve the remaining sauce on the side.

2	(8-ounce) packages light cream cheese, softened
½	cup sugar
¼	cup milk
1	teaspoon vanilla extract
2	eggs
2	tablespoons unsweetened cocoa
1	(9-inch) OREO® Pie Crust (recipe, page 17)
1	(10-ounce) package frozen raspberries in syrup, thawed, pureed and strained

❶ Beat cream cheese, sugar, milk and vanilla in medium bowl with electric mixer at medium speed until smooth. Beat in eggs just until combined.

❷ Transfer 1 cup batter to small bowl; stir in cocoa. Spoon half the chocolate batter into pie crust. Evenly pour white batter over chocolate batter. Top with spoonfuls of remaining chocolate batter. Swirl batters with knife to create a marbled effect.

❸ Bake at 325°F for 35 to 40 minutes or until set. Cool completely on wire rack. Refrigerate at least 4 hours. Serve with pureed raspberries. Makes 6 servings.

Tic-Tac-Toe

Traditional tic-tac-toe is even more fun when you play it with Oreo cookie X's and O's. Draw a large tic-tac-toe grid on a sheet of paper. Then split 10 Oreo cookies, leaving filling on 1 side of each cookie (eat the plain split cookies with milk while playing the game). Use cake decorator gels or icings to write X on filling sides of 5 split cookies and O on filling sides of remaining 5 split cookies.

OREO® Bread Pudding

Prep Time: 10 min. • Bake Time: 45 min.

Transforming bread into a warm, chocolatey pudding is a delicious pleasure.

 4 **cups day-old French bread *or* regular bread cubes**

16 **OREO Chocolate Sandwich Cookies, coarsely broken**

 2 **cups milk**

½ **cup sugar**

¼ **cup butter *or* margarine, melted**

 2 **eggs**

 1 **teaspoon vanilla extract**
     Frozen yogurt *or* whipped cream, optional

❶ Mix bread cubes and broken cookies in large bowl; set aside.

❷ Blend milk, sugar, butter, eggs and vanilla; pour over bread mixture, stirring to coat evenly. Pour into greased 1½-quart round casserole.

❸ Bake at 350°F for 45 to 50 minutes or until set. Serve warm or at room temperature topped with frozen yogurt or whipped cream, if desired. Makes 6 servings.

Oreo Dunkers

If you like dunking Oreo cookies, it's time to dive into some new dunking territory. Here is a list of Oreo Man's favorite choices:

- **Hot chocolate**
- **Milk shakes**
- **Flavored coffees**
- **Marshmallow creme**
- **Butterscotch ice cream topping**
- **Peanut butter**
- **Ice cream**
- **Caramel apple dip**
- **Flavored yogurt**
- **Hot fudge sauce**
- **Thawed frozen whipped topping**
- **Eggnog**
- **Milk, of course!**

Very Berry Parfaits

Very Berry Parfaits

Prep Time: 15 min.

Take advantage of fresh berries from your local farmers' market by preparing these refreshing parfaits. Strawberry- or lemon-flavored yogurt complements the berries especially well.

> **2 cups assorted fresh berries (raspberries, sliced strawberries *and/or* blueberries)**
> **2 (8-ounce) containers low-fat yogurt, any flavor**
> **¼ cup flaked coconut**
> **12 OREO Chocolate Sandwich Cookies, coarsely chopped, divided**
> **Thawed frozen whipped topping, for garnish**
> **Fresh raspberries *or* strawberries, for garnish**

❶ Combine berries, yogurt and coconut in medium bowl.

❷ Set aside ½ cup chopped cookies for garnish. Layer remaining chopped cookies and yogurt mixture in 4 (6- to 8-ounce) parfait glasses or dessert dishes.

❸ Garnish with reserved chopped cookies, whipped topping, raspberries and, if desired, additional cookies. Serve immediately or refrigerate up to 1 hour before serving. Makes 4 servings.

Orange Cream Parfaits

Prep Time: 15 min. • Chill Time: 2 hrs.

If you don't have parfait glasses on hand, make one large dessert by layering the gelatin mixture and cookies in a 1-quart glass bowl.

> **12 OREO DOUBLE STUF Chocolate Sandwich Cookies, divided**
> **1 (4-serving-size) package ROYAL Orange Gelatin**
> **1 cup boiling water**
> **1 pint vanilla ice cream, softened**
> **Thawed frozen whipped topping, for garnish**

❶ Coarsely chop 8 cookies; set aside.

❷ Dissolve gelatin in boiling water; stir in ice cream until melted. If necessary, refrigerate 5 minutes or until slightly thickened.

❸ Layer gelatin mixture and chopped cookies in 4 (8-ounce) parfait glasses or dessert dishes. Refrigerate 2 hours or until firm.

❹ Garnish with whipped topping and remaining 4 cookies. Makes 4 servings.

Cookie Pancakes

Prep Time: 20 min. • Cook Time: 15 min.

For extra convenience, cook the pancakes in advance. Then cool, wrap tightly and refrigerate for up to 2 days or freeze for up to 1 month. Thaw and reheat the pancakes in the microwave oven just before serving.

1	**cup pancake mix**
¾	**cup milk**
1	**egg**
2	**teaspoons vegetable oil**
12	**OREO Chocolate Sandwich Cookies, finely chopped, divided**
1½	**cups sliced bananas**
1½	**cups sliced fresh strawberries**
	Vanilla frozen yogurt
	Strawberry syrup

❶ Mix pancake mix, milk, egg and oil just until blended; stir in 1 cup chopped cookies.

❷ Heat a lightly greased griddle or skillet over medium-high heat. Spoon batter by teaspoons onto griddle. Cook until bubbly; turn and cook until lightly browned. Keep warm until serving time.

❸ Place 6 pancakes on each serving plate. Top with bananas, strawberries, remaining chopped cookies and frozen yogurt. Drizzle with strawberry syrup. Serve immediately. Makes 6 servings (36 silver-dollar-size pancakes).

OREO® Pie Crust

Prep Time: 10 min.

Here's an easy-to-make homemade crust that'll add the fabulous taste of Oreo cookies to all of your favorite no-bake pies. But if you're short on time, look for the already prepared Oreo Pie Crust in your supermarket.

22 OREO Chocolate Sandwich Cookies, finely crushed

¼ cup butter *or* margarine, melted

❶ Mix crushed cookies and butter in medium bowl. Press firmly on bottom and side of 9-inch pie plate.

❷ Fill with your favorite no-bake filling. Refrigerate or freeze before serving, if needed. Makes 1 (9-inch) crust.

Coconut Cookie Crust: Prepare OREO® Pie Crust as directed, except stir ½ cup toasted coconut into crushed cookie mixture.

Nutty Cookie Crust: Prepare OREO® Pie Crust as directed, except stir ⅓ cup finely chopped toasted PLANTERS Walnuts *or* Pecans into crushed cookie mixture.

Peanut Butter Cookie Crust: Prepare OREO® Pie Crust as directed, except substitute ⅓ cup creamy peanut butter (do not melt) for butter *or* margarine.

The Oreo Flip Game

With a little practice, you'll amaze your friends. To play, bend your arm back so your hand is palm side up behind your ear. Stack one or two Oreo cookies on your arm, just above your elbow, so they rest flat. With one quick, strong motion, bring your hand straight up from your ear and down to your side. As you do so, catch the cookies as they fall off your elbow.

Velvet Chocolate Cheesecake

Velvet Chocolate Cheesecake

Prep Time: 30 min. • Bake Time: 40 min. plus cooling • Chill Time: 4 hrs.

To quickly soften the cream cheese for this cheesecake, unwrap an 8-ounce package and place it on a microwavable plate. Microwave on HIGH (100% power) for 45 to 60 seconds.

 38 **OREO Chocolate Sandwich Cookies, divided**
  5 **tablespoons butter *or* margarine, melted**
  5 **ounces semisweet chocolate, divided**
  1 **(8-ounce) package cream cheese, softened**
 ½ **cup *plus* 2 tablespoons sugar, divided**
1½ **cups dairy sour cream, divided**
  2 **eggs**
  1 **teaspoon vanilla extract**
    Fresh raspberries, mint sprigs *and* chocolate curls,* for garnish

❶ Finely crush 24 cookies; mix crushed cookies and butter in bowl. Press firmly on bottom of 9-inch springform pan. Stand remaining 14 cookies around edge of pan, pressing firmly into crumb mixture. Set aside.

❷ Melt 4 ounces chocolate in small saucepan over low heat; set aside.

❸ Beat cream cheese and ½ cup sugar with electric mixer at medium speed until creamy. Beat in ½ cup sour cream, eggs and vanilla until smooth. Blend in melted chocolate. Pour into prepared crust.

❹ Bake at 325°F for 35 to 40 minutes or until cheesecake is slightly puffed and center is set. Blend remaining 1 cup sour cream and 2 tablespoons sugar; spread over cheesecake. Bake 5 minutes more. Cool to room temperature.

❺ Melt remaining 1 ounce chocolate; drizzle over cheesecake. Refrigerate at least 4 hours. Garnish with raspberries, mint and chocolate curls. Makes 12 to 14 servings.

*Note: To make chocolate curls, let a bar of dark and/or white chocolate come to room temperature. Carefully draw a vegetable peeler at an angle across the chocolate.

OREO® Ice Cream Tartufo

Prep Time: 30 min. • Freeze Time: 3 hrs.

TARTUFO (tahr-TOO-foh) is the Italian word for truffle, and these chocolate balls of Oreo and fudge-coated ice cream resemble giant ones! Keep plenty on hand in your freezer for an impressive dessert that's ready in minutes.

1½   **pints chocolate ice cream**

15   **OREO Chocolate Sandwich Cookies, finely chopped**

1⅓ **cups semisweet chocolate chips***

4   **teaspoons vegetable oil***

1   **(10-ounce) package frozen raspberries in syrup, thawed,**
pureed and strained

Fresh raspberries, for garnish

❶ Using a ½-cup ice cream scoop, scoop ice cream into 6 balls; roll in chopped cookies. Place on waxed-paper-lined baking sheet; cover and freeze at least 2 hours or until firm.

❷ Heat chocolate chips and oil in small saucepan over low heat, stirring until melted and smooth. Cool. Place ice cream balls on wire rack. Ladle 2 tablespoons melted chocolate over each ball, coating the top and sides. Freeze at least 1 hour or until firm.

❸ Spoon raspberry sauce into dessert dishes or onto serving plates. Cut each tartufo in half or quarters; arrange on top of sauce. Garnish with raspberries. Serve immediately. Makes 6 servings.

*Note: If you like, substitute ¾ cup chocolate-flavored hard-shell topping for the melted chocolate and oil mixture.

OREO® Ice Cream Tartufo

Towering Brownie Pyramids

Prep Time: 30 min. • Bake Time: 28 min. plus cooling • Freeze Time: 3 hrs.

This luscious ice cream sandwich, in the shape of an elegant triangle, makes the ideal dessert for a summer party.

- 18 **OREO Chocolate Sandwich Cookies, divided**
- 1 **(19.8-ounce) package fudge brownie mix**
- ½ **cup vegetable oil**
- ¼ **cup water**
- 2 **eggs**
- 1 **pint ice cream, any flavor, softened**
-    **Chocolate-flavored syrup *or* chocolate-flavored hard-shell topping, for garnish**

❶ Coarsely chop 14 cookies. Prepare brownie mix according to package directions using oil, water and eggs; stir in chopped cookies. Spread batter into foil-lined and greased 13x9x2-inch baking pan.

❷ Bake at 350°F for 28 to 30 minutes or until toothpick inserted 2 inches from side comes out almost clean. Cool in pan on wire rack.

❸ Cut brownie in half crosswise. Place 1 brownie half, upside down, on waxed-paper-lined baking sheet. Spread ice cream over brownie to edges; top with remaining brownie half. Wrap with plastic wrap; freeze 3 to 4 hours or until firm.

❹ Cut into 4 (4½x3¼-inch) rectangles; halve rectangles diagonally to form 8 triangles. Stand each triangle on its side on a serving plate. Halve remaining 4 cookies. Garnish triangles with cookie halves and chocolate syrup. Serve immediately or freeze until serving time. Makes 8 servings.

Hot Fudge Sundae Dessert

Prep Time: 30 min. • Freeze Time: 4 hrs. and 40 min.

Complete with cherries on top, this dessert is made with a trio of ice cream flavors. Substitute any ice cream flavors you like for those suggested here.

26 OREO Chocolate Sandwich Cookies, finely crushed

5 tablespoons butter *or* margarine, melted

1 quart chocolate *or* vanilla ice cream, softened, divided

1 cup hot fudge sauce, warmed, divided

1 pint strawberry ice cream

1 pint coffee ice cream

1 cup whipped cream *or* thawed frozen whipped topping

¼ cup PLANTERS Walnuts

Maraschino cherries with stems, for garnish

❶ Mix crushed cookies and butter in bowl. Press firmly on bottom and 2 inches up side of 9-inch springform pan. Freeze 10 minutes.

❷ Spread half the chocolate ice cream into prepared crust. Top with ⅔ cup fudge sauce; freeze 30 minutes. Spread with remaining half of chocolate ice cream.

❸ Scoop strawberry and coffee ice cream into balls; arrange on cake. Freeze 4 hours or until firm.

❹ Drizzle remaining fudge sauce over cake. Top with whipped cream and walnuts; garnish with cherries. Serve immediately. Makes 12 servings.

Oreo Rollers

Dress up the edges of Oreo® cookies by making Oreo Rollers! Place a generous spoonful of peanut butter, thawed frozen whipped topping or canned frosting on a paper plate, spreading it out slightly. Spoon miniature candy-coated semisweet chocolate chips, colored sprinkles, chopped nuts or other treats on the same plate. Roll Oreo cookie edges first in peanut butter, whipped topping or frosting, then through the treats. Fun and delicious!

German Chocolate Cake

Prep Time: 20 min. • Bake Time: 25 min. plus cooling

If you're a fan of classic German chocolate cake, you'll love this streamlined Oreo® version. For the chocolate lover in your crowd, substitute chocolate frosting for the vanilla.

 1   **(18.25-ounce) package German chocolate *or* devil's food cake mix**
1¼   **cups water**
 ½   **cup vegetable oil**
 3   **eggs**
 1   **(16-ounce) can vanilla frosting**
 ¾   **cup flaked coconut**
 ¾   **cup PLANTERS Pecans, chopped**
 ⅓   **cup thick caramel ice cream topping**
12   **OREO Chocolate Sandwich Cookies, finely chopped**

❶ Mix cake mix, water, oil and eggs in large bowl with electric mixer at low speed until moistened. Beat 2 minutes at medium speed. Pour into 2 greased and floured 9-inch round cake pans.

❷ Bake at 350°F for 25 to 35 minutes or until toothpick inserted near center comes out clean. Cool in pans on wire racks 10 minutes; remove from pans. Cool completely.

❸ Mix frosting, coconut, pecans and caramel topping. Place 1 cake layer on serving plate; spread with half the frosting mixture. Top with ½ cup chopped cookies, pressing gently into frosting.

❹ Top with remaining cake layer; spread top with remaining frosting mixture. Sprinkle with remaining chopped cookies, pressing gently into frosting. Makes 12 servings.

German Chocolate Cake

Mocha Cream Pie

Prep Time: 20 min. • Bake/Cook Time: 10 min.
Chill Time: 20 min. • Freeze Time: 4 hrs.

You'll find this triple-chocolate pie embellished with coffee ice cream simply delicious!

40	**OREO Chocolate Sandwich Cookies, divided**
6	**tablespoons butter *or* margarine, divided**
8	**ounces milk chocolate, finely chopped**
¼	**cup heavy cream**
2	**tablespoons strong brewed coffee**
1	**(12-ounce) container frozen whipped topping, thawed, divided**
1	**tablespoon chocolate-flavored syrup**

❶ Finely crush 20 cookies; set aside. Coarsely chop 12 cookies; set aside.

❷ Melt 3 tablespoons butter. Mix finely crushed cookies and melted butter in bowl. Press firmly on bottom and up side of 9-inch pie plate. Bake at 350°F for 5 minutes. Cool.

❸ Heat chocolate, heavy cream, remaining 3 tablespoons butter and coffee in large saucepan over medium-low heat, stirring until chocolate and butter melt. Remove from heat; stir in coarsely chopped cookies. Refrigerate 20 minutes.

❹ Fold half the whipped topping into chocolate mixture until well blended. Spread into prepared crust; freeze 4 hours or until firm.

❺ Whisk remaining half of whipped topping and chocolate syrup in bowl until well combined. Spread pie with whipped topping mixture; garnish with remaining 8 cookies. Makes 8 servings.

Fun Fact

How much creme filling is inside all the Oreo® cookies eaten in one year? Well, if you used it to frost cakes, it would cover all of the wedding cakes served in the United States for two years—that's about 4,724,000 three-tier cakes!

OREO® Peanut Butter Pie

Prep Time: 15 min. • Chill Time: 4 hrs.

Toasted peanuts are the crowning touch for this dessert. To toast peanuts, spread them in a single layer in a baking pan. Bake at 350°F for 5 to 10 minutes or until light golden, stirring once or twice.

1	**(3-ounce) package cream cheese, softened**
⅔	**cup sugar**
⅔	**cup creamy peanut butter**
2	**tablespoons milk**
2	**cups thawed frozen whipped topping**
18	**OREO Chocolate Sandwich Cookies, coarsely chopped, divided**
1	**(9-inch) OREO® Pie Crust (recipe, page 17)**
2	**tablespoons PLANTERS COCKTAIL Peanuts, chopped, toasted**

❶ Beat cream cheese and sugar in large bowl with electric mixer at medium speed until creamy.

❷ Add peanut butter and milk; beat 2 minutes more or until smooth.

❸ Fold in whipped topping and 1¾ cups chopped cookies. Spread into pie crust. Sprinkle with remaining chopped cookies and peanuts. Refrigerate 4 to 6 hours or overnight. Makes 8 servings.

OREO® Strawberry Shortcake

OREO® Strawberry Shortcake

Prep Time: 20 min. • Bake Time: 25 min. plus cooling

For a party or special-occasion dessert, bake the Oreo-speckled cake layers in advance, wrap them tightly and freeze for up to 1 month.

 1 **(18.25-ounce) package yellow cake mix**
1¼ **cups water**
 ¼ **cup vegetable oil**
 3 **eggs**
16 **OREO Chocolate Sandwich Cookies, coarsely chopped, divided**
 2 **cups sliced fresh strawberries**
 3 **cups sweetened whipped cream*** *or* **thawed frozen whipped topping**
    Fresh strawberries *and* **edible flower, for garnish**

❶ Mix cake mix, water, oil and eggs in large bowl with electric mixer at low speed until moistened. Beat 2 minutes at medium speed. Stir in ½ cup chopped cookies. Pour into 2 greased and floured 9-inch round cake pans.

❷ Bake at 350°F for 25 to 35 minutes or until toothpick inserted near center comes out clean. Cool in pans on wire racks 10 minutes; remove from pans. Cool completely.

❸ Fold ¾ cup chopped cookies and sliced strawberries into whipped cream in large bowl. Place 1 cake layer on serving plate; spread with half the whipped cream mixture. Top with remaining cake layer; spread top with remaining half of whipped cream mixture.

❹ Garnish with strawberries, flower and remaining chopped cookies. Makes 12 servings.

*Note: To make sweetened whipped cream, beat 1½ cups heavy cream, 3 tablespoons sugar and 1 teaspoon vanilla extract in chilled bowl with electric mixer at medium speed until soft peaks form.

OREO® Mint Ice Cream Dessert

Prep Time: 20 min. • Freeze Time: 4 hrs. and 10 min.

This after-dinner mint dessert is the perfect choice for a large dinner party. It's easy to make and can be made days ahead.

> 1 **(1-pound 4-ounce) package OREO Chocolate Sandwich Cookies, divided**
> ¼ **cup butter or margarine, melted**
> ½ **gallon mint chocolate chip ice cream, softened**

❶ Set aside 15 cookies; finely chop remaining cookies. Mix chopped cookies and butter in bowl. Press firmly on bottom of 13x9x2-inch baking pan. Freeze 10 minutes.

❷ Spread ice cream evenly over crust. Place reserved cookies evenly on ice cream so each piece will have 1 whole cookie, pressing firmly into ice cream. Freeze at least 4 hours or overnight. Makes 15 servings.

Dalmatian Delight

Prep Time: 25 min. • Chill Time: 3 hrs.

Both the Oreo-spotted cream-cheese filling and the cookie "paw" garnish lend cute canine appeal to this easy, no-bake pie.

> 38 **OREO Chocolate Sandwich Cookies, divided**
> ¼ **cup butter or margarine, melted**
> 1 **(8-ounce) package cream cheese, softened**
> ½ **cup sugar**
> ½ **cup heavy cream, whipped**
> 24 **semisweet chocolate chips**

❶ Finely crush 20 cookies. Mix crushed cookies and butter in bowl. Press firmly on the bottom and up side of 9-inch pie plate; set aside.

❷ Coarsely chop 12 cookies; set aside. Beat cream cheese and sugar in medium bowl with electric mixer at medium speed until creamy. Fold in whipped cream and chopped cookies. Spread mixture into prepared crust. Refrigerate 3 hours.

❸ To serve, cut pie into 6 wedges. Place 1 reserved cookie in center of each slice to make a "paw." Place 4 chocolate chips, point side down, along one edge of each cookie to make "toes." Makes 6 servings.

OREO® Banana Split Pie

Prep Time: 20 min. • Freeze Time: 1½ hrs.

Luscious layers of chocolate and strawberry ice cream, hot fudge sauce, Oreo cookies, whipped topping and bananas form an incredibly decadent pie (photo, page 5).

> 12 **OREO Chocolate Sandwich Cookies, divided**
> 1 **pint chocolate ice cream, softened**
> 1 **(9-inch) OREO® Pie Crust (recipe, page 17)**
> ¾ **cup hot fudge sauce, warmed, divided**
> 2 **bananas, sliced, divided**
> 1 **pint strawberry ice cream, softened**
> **Thawed frozen whipped topping, for garnish**
> **Maraschino cherries with stems, for garnish**

❶ Finely chop 8 cookies; set aside. Halve remaining 4 cookies; set aside.

❷ Spread chocolate ice cream into pie crust. Freeze 30 minutes or until ice cream is firm.

❸ Drizzle half the fudge sauce over ice cream. Top with finely chopped cookies and half the banana slices.

❹ Carefully spread strawberry ice cream over banana slices. Stand cookie halves around edge of pie. Top with remaining fudge sauce and remaining banana slices. Freeze at least 1 hour or until firm.

❺ Garnish with whipped topping, cherries and, if desired, additional cookies just before serving. Makes 8 servings.

Oreo Hockey

To play **Oreo Hockey**, at one end of a table, line up two Oreo cookies for the goal. Using your finger, flick another cookie from the other end of the table toward the goal. On each turn, each player flicks a cookie toward the goal. If any of the cookies touch each other, your turn ends and your opponent plays. The first person to flick a cookie through the goal, without it falling off the table, wins!

OREO® Fruit Tart

Prep Time: 15 min. • Chill Time: 2 hrs.

Besides being a delightful after-dinner dessert, this shimmering fruit tart makes a lovely addition to a brunch or luncheon menu.

 1 **(8-ounce) package light cream cheese, softened**
¼ **cup sugar**
 2 **cups thawed frozen whipped topping**
 1 **(9-inch) OREO® Pie Crust (recipe, page 17)**
 4 **OREO Chocolate Sandwich Cookies, finely chopped**
1½ **to 2 cups assorted fresh fruit (sliced kiwifruit, sliced mango**
     ***and/or* halved strawberries)**
 2 **tablespoons apricot preserves, melted**

❶ Beat cream cheese and sugar in bowl with electric mixer at medium speed for 1 minute or until smooth.

❷ Fold in whipped topping; spread into pie crust.

❸ Top with chopped cookies and fruit. Brush preserves over fruit with pastry brush. Refrigerate 2 hours or until serving time. Makes 8 servings.

OREO® Fruit Tart

Sweet Cannoli Pie

Prep Time: 15 min. • Chill Time: 3½ hrs.

This irresistible pie is reminiscent of the wonderful Italian dessert cannoli, which features crisp pastry shells filled with a sweetened ricotta filling and accented with bits of chocolate and candied citron.

1 envelope **KNOX Unflavored Gelatine**

¾ **cup milk, divided**

1 **(15-ounce) container ricotta cheese**

½ **cup sugar**

1 **teaspoon vanilla extract**

1 **teaspoon grated orange peel**

9 **OREO Chocolate Sandwich Cookies, divided**

1 **(9-inch) OREO® Pie Crust (recipe, page 17)**

Whipped cream *and* orange slices, for garnish

❶ Sprinkle gelatine over ¼ cup cold milk in small saucepan; let stand 1 minute. Cook over low heat for 3 minutes, stirring until gelatine completely dissolves.

❷ Blend ricotta, remaining ½ cup milk, sugar, vanilla and orange peel in electric blender or food processor until smooth. Gradually add gelatine mixture while blending (or through feed cap while processing) until blended. Pour into large bowl and refrigerate, stirring occasionally, 30 to 45 minutes or until mixture mounds slightly when dropped from spoon.

❸ Coarsely chop 6 cookies; fold into cream mixture. Spread into pie crust. Refrigerate 3 hours or until firm.

❹ Halve remaining 3 cookies; garnish pie with whipped cream, cookie halves and orange slices. Makes 6 servings.

OREO® Celebration Cake

Prep Time: 15 min. • Bake Time: 25 min. plus cooling

Celebrate an Oreo lover's birthday with this fun-to-eat cake. Not only does it have cookies baked right into the chocolate layers, but it's also decorated to resemble a giant Oreo cookie!

1	**(18.25-ounce) package devil's food cake mix**
1⅓	**cups water**
½	**cup vegetable oil**
3	**eggs**
20	**OREO Chocolate Sandwich Cookies, coarsely chopped, divided**
1	**(16-ounce) can vanilla frosting, divided**
4	**ounces semisweet chocolate**
1	**tablespoon butter *or* margarine**

❶ Mix cake mix, water, oil and eggs in large bowl with electric mixer at low speed until moistened. Beat 2 minutes at medium speed. Stir in 1½ cups chopped cookies. Pour into 2 greased and floured 9-inch round cake pans.

❷ Bake at 350°F for 25 to 35 minutes or until toothpick inserted near center comes out clean. Cool in pans on wire racks 10 minutes; remove from pans. Cool completely.

❸ Reserve ⅓ cup frosting for garnish. Place 1 cake layer on serving plate; spread with remaining frosting. Top with remaining chopped cookies, pressing gently into frosting. Top with remaining cake layer.

❹ Heat chocolate and butter in small saucepan over low heat, stirring until melted and smooth. Cool slightly and spread evenly over top of cake. Cool 10 minutes or until glaze is set. Garnish with reserved frosting to resemble a large Oreo cookie. Makes 12 servings.

Sweet Snacking

Whether you're longing for a midday treat or a late-evening snack, here you'll find everything from Fruit 'n' Nutty Snack Mix you can enjoy as a quick energy boost to OREO® Biscotti for savoring with a cup of tea after the kids have gone to bed.

OREO® Biscotti (recipe, page 39)
Crunchy Dipped Strawberries (recipe, page 38)

Crunchy Dipped Strawberries

Prep Time: 20 min. plus standing • Cook Time: 5 min.

When purchasing fresh strawberries to make these candied berries, choose bright-colored ones with green caps and a strong strawberry fragrance (photo, page 37).

  8   **ounces semisweet *and/or* white chocolate**
  5   **tablespoons butter *or* margarine**
  1   **pint fresh strawberries, washed, well dried**
 12   **OREO Chocolate Sandwich Cookies, finely chopped**

❶ Heat chocolate and butter in medium saucepan over low heat, stirring until melted and smooth.

❷ Dip strawberries into melted chocolate; roll in chopped cookies.

❸ Place on waxed-paper-lined baking sheet; let stand until chocolate sets. Store in refrigerator for up to 24 hours. Makes 1 pint.

Crunchy Dipped Pretzels: Prepare Crunchy Dipped Strawberries as directed, except substitute 1 (10¼-ounce) package pretzel rods for berries. Coat one-third of each pretzel rod with chocolate; roll in chopped cookies. Store in airtight container.

OREO® Biscotti

Prep Time: 30 min. • Bake Time: 45 min. plus cooling

These crunchy, easy-to-make biscotti are generously studded with Oreo chunks. Dunk them in your favorite flavored coffee or OREO® Mint Cocoa (recipe, page 55) for an incredible taste treat (photo, page 37).

1	**cup sugar**
⅓	**cup butter** *or* **margarine, melted**
3	**eggs**
2	**teaspoons vanilla extract**
3	**cups all-purpose flour**
1½	**teaspoons DAVIS Baking Powder**
¼	**teaspoon salt**
16	**OREO Chocolate Sandwich Cookies, coarsely chopped**
2	**ounces semisweet** *and/or* **white chocolate, melted, optional**

❶ Beat sugar, butter, eggs and vanilla in large bowl with electric mixer at medium speed until blended. Stir in flour, baking powder and salt. Fold in chopped cookies.

❷ Divide mixture in half. With floured hands, shape each half into a 9x3-inch loaf on a lightly greased large baking sheet.

❸ Bake at 350°F for 25 to 30 minutes or until golden brown and toothpick inserted in centers comes out clean. Remove from oven; cool 10 minutes. Cut each loaf diagonally into 15 (½-inch-thick) slices. Place slices, cut side up, on same baking sheet. Bake 10 to 12 minutes more on each side or until lightly toasted. Cool completely on wire racks.

❹ Drizzle tops with melted chocolate, if desired. Makes 2½ dozen.

Fun Fact

Dunking Oreo cookies in milk is just one of the many popular ways to eat them. If every Oreo cookie eaten in one year was actually dunked in milk, cows would have to work lots of overtime. It would take about 42 million extra gallons of milk to accommodate all of those additional milk dunks! Cowabunga!!

OREO® Candy Bark

Prep Time: 10 min. plus cooling • Cook Time: 5 min.

Pack pieces of this colorful candy bark in snack-size plastic bags to give as favors at a child's party. Or, tuck them inside a pretty tin and take as a hostess gift to a dinner party.

> **16**   **OREO *or* OREO DOUBLE STUF Chocolate Sandwich Cookies, coarsely chopped**
>
> **1½**   **cups PLANTERS Mini Pretzel Twists**
>
> **⅓**   **cup raisins *or* dried cranberries**
>
> **12**   **ounces white chocolate**
>
>   **Colored sprinkles, optional**

❶ Mix chopped cookies, pretzels and raisins in medium bowl; set aside.

❷ Heat chocolate in medium saucepan over low heat, stirring until melted and smooth.

❸ Pour melted chocolate quickly over cookie mixture, tossing to coat evenly. Spread in single layer on lightly greased baking sheet. Top with colored sprinkles, if desired, pressing gently into mixture.

❹ Cool until firm; break into pieces. Store in airtight container. Makes about 1½ pounds.

Oreo Art

In addition to traditional art supplies, give your budding Van Goghs an Oreo cookie! The textured cookie is perfect for creating all sorts of artistic rubbings. Have your youngsters use crayons or colored pencils with different papers, such as typing paper, computer paper or tissue paper. Then, encourage them to create abstract designs. Or, get their imaginations rolling to make Oreo portraits, buildings, animals, monsters, cars and landscapes.

OREO® Ice Cream Sandwiches

Prep Time: 15 min. • Freeze Time: 30 min.

For variety, use assorted flavors of ice cream or sherbet in these miniature frosty delights.

15 OREO Chocolate Sandwich Cookies, divided
6 tablespoons ice cream *or* sherbet, slightly softened

❶ Finely chop 3 cookies; set aside.

❷ Spoon 1 tablespoon ice cream or sherbet onto each of 6 cookies; top with remaining 6 cookies to form sandwiches.

❸ Quickly roll in chopped cookies. Place on waxed-paper-lined baking sheet; freeze 30 minutes or until firm. Wrap in plastic wrap to store in freezer. Makes 6 ice cream sandwiches.

OREO® Ice Cream Sandwiches

Chocolate Volcano Cupcakes

Prep Time: 20 min. • Bake Time: 20 min. plus cooling

Erupting with frosting "lava," these little cakes are sure to be explosively good at any gathering!

1	**(18.25-ounce) package devil's food cake mix**
1¼	**cups water**
½	**cup vegetable oil**
3	**eggs**
16	**OREO Chocolate Sandwich Cookies, coarsely chopped**
1	**(16-ounce) can vanilla frosting**

❶ Mix cake mix, water, oil and eggs in large bowl with electric mixer at low speed until moistened. Beat 2 minutes at medium speed. Stir in chopped cookies. Spoon into 24 paper-lined or lightly greased 2½-inch muffin pan cups.

❷ Bake at 350°F for 20 to 25 minutes or until toothpick inserted near centers comes out clean. Cool in muffin pans on wire racks 5 minutes. Remove from pans; cool completely.

❸ Fill pastry bag, fitted with rosette tip, with frosting. Insert tip slightly into tops of cupcakes and squeeze gently to fill cupcakes.* Makes 24 cupcakes.

*Note: Cupcakes also can be filled by poking a hole in center of cupcakes with tip of spoon. In place of a pastry bag and tip, fill plastic food storage bag with frosting; cut off one corner point and squeeze gently to fill cupcakes.

Chocolate Volcano
Cupcakes

Crunchy Banana Bread

Prep Time: 15 min. • Bake Time: 45 min. plus cooling

Chock-full of crunchy Oreo cookies, this delectable banana bread tastes great any time of day. Enjoy it with a cup of coffee for breakfast, with a glass of milk as a mid-afternoon snack or with a scoop of ice cream for dessert.

- 1 **(14-ounce) package banana quick bread mix**
- 1 **cup water**
- 3 **tablespoons vegetable oil**
- 2 **eggs**
- 16 **OREO Chocolate Sandwich Cookies, coarsely chopped**

❶ Prepare bread mix according to package directions using water, oil and eggs; stir in chopped cookies. Pour batter into greased 9x5x3-inch loaf pan.

❷ Bake at 350°F for 45 to 50 minutes or until toothpick inserted in center comes out clean. Cool in pan on wire rack 10 minutes. Remove from pan; cool completely. Makes 10 servings.

Cookie Granola Topping

Prep Time: 10 min. • Bake Time: 25 min. plus cooling

Keep plenty of this crispy granola on hand to top ice cream or canned fruit, or to simply munch on as a satisfying snack.

- 2 **cups rolled oats**
- ½ **cup flaked coconut**
- ½ **cup PLANTERS Pecans, coarsely chopped**
- 3 **tablespoons honey**
- 4 **teaspoons orange juice**
- 16 **OREO Chocolate Sandwich Cookies, coarsely chopped**

❶ Mix oats, coconut, pecans, honey and orange juice in 15½x10½x1-inch baking pan.

❷ Bake at 300°F for 15 minutes; stir. Bake 10 minutes more. Cool.

❸ Stir chopped cookies into oat mixture. Store in airtight container. Serve as a topping for ice cream, yogurt or pudding. Makes 5 cups.

OREO® Ripple Coffee Cake

OREO® Ripple Coffee Cake

Prep Time: 20 min. • Bake Time: 45 min. plus cooling

This luscious coffee cake can double as a fabulous dessert. If you like, omit the powdered sugar icing and serve with dollops of whipped topping and fresh berries.

24	OREO Chocolate Sandwich Cookies, coarsely chopped
⅓	cup all-purpose flour
¼	cup butter *or* margarine, melted
⅓	cup miniature semisweet chocolate chips
1	(16-ounce) package yellow pound cake mix
¾	cup water
2	eggs
1	cup powdered sugar
4	teaspoons milk
	Orange slices *and* fresh raspberries, for garnish

❶ Mix chopped cookies, flour and butter. Stir in chocolate chips; set aside.

❷ Prepare cake mix according to package directions using water and eggs. Pour half the batter into greased 9- or 10-inch tube pan. Sprinkle 2 cups cookie mixture evenly over batter. Top with remaining batter and cookie mixture, pressing cookie mixture gently into batter.

❸ Bake at 350°F for 45 to 50 minutes or until toothpick inserted near center comes out clean. Cool in pan on wire rack 10 minutes. Remove from pan; invert cake. Cool completely.

❹ Mix powdered sugar and milk; drizzle over cake. Garnish with orange slices and fresh raspberries. Makes 12 servings.

Fruit 'n' Nutty Snack Mix

Prep Time: 5 min.

Stow this scrumptious fruit-and-nut snack in your backpack to nibble on while hiking along the trail or taking a road trip in the car.

16	OREO *or* OREO DOUBLE STUF Chocolate Sandwich Cookies, coarsely broken
1	cup macadamia nuts, cashews *or* peanuts
1	cup dried cranberries

❶ Mix broken cookies, nuts and cranberries in large bowl.

❷ Serve immediately or store in airtight container. Makes 4 cups.

OREO® Crunch Bars

OREO® Crunch Bars

Prep Time: 15 min. • Bake Time: 15 min.

Both young and old alike will enjoy these sweet treats made with gooey marshmallow filling snuggled between two layers of chopped Oreo cookies.

> **34 OREO Chocolate Sandwich Cookies, divided**
> ¼ **cup butter *or* margarine, melted**
> 1 **(7½-ounce) jar marshmallow creme**
> ½ **cup semisweet chocolate chips**
> ⅓ **cup PLANTERS Walnuts, chopped**

❶ Coarsely chop 8 cookies; set aside. Finely crush remaining 26 cookies. Mix finely crushed cookies and butter in bowl. Press firmly on bottom of greased 8x8x2- or 9x9x2-inch baking pan.

❷ Dollop marshmallow creme over crust to within ½ inch of edges. Sprinkle chips, nuts and chopped cookies over marshmallow layer, pressing gently.

❸ Bake at 350°F for 15 to 18 minutes or until marshmallow creme puffs slightly. Cool completely in pan on wire rack. Cut into triangles or squares to serve. Makes 16 servings.

Chocolate Peanut Butter Frogs

Prep Time: 20 min. plus standing • Cook Time: 5 min.

There are a myriad of ways to serve these adorable cookie "frogs": as a classroom or lunch box treat, a birthday party favor or decoration on top of a green-frosted "lily pad" cupcake, to name just a few.

2	**ounces semisweet chocolate**
2	**tablespoons butter *or* margarine**
12	**OREO Chocolate Sandwich Cookies**
3	**tablespoons creamy peanut butter**
24	**PLANTERS Mini Pretzels Twists**
24	**candy-coated chocolate *or* peanut butter candies**

❶ Heat chocolate and butter in small saucepan over low heat, stirring until melted and smooth; set aside.

❷ Spread bottom of each cookie with 1 teaspoon peanut butter; dip bottom into melted chocolate mixture. Quickly press 2 pretzel twists on chocolate for frog legs with wide part of pretzels facing outward. Place, pretzel side down, on waxed-paper-lined baking sheet.

❸ Attach candies for eyes using remaining chocolate mixture or, if desired, additional peanut butter. Let stand until chocolate sets. Makes 12 cookie frogs.

Chocolate
Peanut Butter Frogs

OREO® Muffins

Prep Time: 25 min. • Bake Time: 15 min.

Topped with a crumbled cookie streusel, these cake-like muffins make a terrific lunch box or after-school snack for kids.

1¾	**cups all-purpose flour**
¼	**cup sugar**
1	**tablespoon DAVIS Baking Powder**
⅓	**cup butter *or* margarine**
1	**cup milk**
1	**egg**
16	**OREO Chocolate Sandwich Cookies, coarsely chopped**
½	**cup miniature semisweet chocolate chips, optional**
	Cookie Crumb Topping (recipe follows)

❶ Mix flour, sugar and baking powder in medium bowl; cut in butter until mixture resembles coarse crumbs.

❷ Blend milk and egg in small bowl; stir into flour mixture. Gently stir in chopped cookies and, if desired, chocolate chips; do not overmix. Spoon batter into 12 greased or paper-lined 2½-inch muffin pan cups.

❸ Sprinkle with Cookie Crumb Topping.

❹ Bake at 400°F for 15 to 20 minutes or until toothpick inserted near centers comes out clean. Cool in pan on wire rack 5 minutes. Remove from pan; cool slightly. Serve warm. Makes 12 muffins.

Cookie Crumb Topping: Mix 5 finely chopped OREO cookies and 3 tablespoons each of all-purpose flour and sugar. Blend in 2 tablespoons softened butter *or* margarine until crumbly.

Oreo Wheelies

Include Oreo cookies for lunch so your kids can play the lunchtime Oreo Wheelies game. Players see how far they can roll an Oreo cookie on its edge, like a wheel, before it falls down. For extra fun, they can use a ruler or tape measure to measure the distances rolled in three attempts, then add them up—the person with the highest score wins!

Mini Marbled Cheesecakes

Prep Time: 20 min. • Bake Time: 20 min. plus cooling

You'll win rave reviews when you bring these dainty cheesecakes to your next potluck supper. For an extra-special touch, garnish each cheesecake with a sprig of fresh mint.

- **24 OREO Chocolate Sandwich Cookies, divided**
- **2 (8-ounce) packages cream cheese, softened**
- **½ cup sugar**
- **2 eggs**
- **1 teaspoon vanilla extract**
- **2 ounces semisweet chocolate, melted, cooled**
- **Thawed frozen whipped topping, for garnish**

❶ Place 1 cookie in bottom of each of 16 paper-lined 2½-inch muffin pan cups; set aside.

❷ Beat cream cheese, sugar, eggs and vanilla in large bowl with electric mixer at medium speed for 3 minutes or until smooth. Reserve ½ cup batter. Spoon remaining batter into prepared muffin cups.

❸ Blend reserved batter and melted chocolate. Spoon about 1 teaspoon chocolate batter onto white batter in each cup. Swirl batters with knife to create a marbled effect.

❹ Bake at 350°F for 20 to 25 minutes or until filling is set and slightly puffed. Cool. Refrigerate until serving time. Halve remaining 8 cookies. Garnish cheesecakes with whipped topping and halved cookies. Makes 16 mini cheesecakes.

Holiday
Magic
~

Whether it's a traditional holiday, such as Halloween or Christmas, or simply greeting the first blossoms of spring, there's reason to celebrate. Set the stage for all of your gatherings by serving this magical collection of seasonal sweets.

Pumpkin Patch Ice Cream Dessert (recipe, page 52)
Halloween Cupcakes (recipe, page 53)

Pumpkin Patch Ice Cream Dessert

Prep Time: 30 min. • Freeze Time: 3 hrs.

To enjoy this luscious dessert (photo, page 51) at Easter, simply use the Spring Oreo® cookies and decorate with seasonal candies.

32	**Halloween OREO Chocolate Sandwich Cookies, divided**
3	**tablespoons butter *or* margarine, melted**
1	**tablespoon sugar**
1	**quart chocolate ice cream, softened**
1	**quart vanilla ice cream, softened**
1½	**cups thawed frozen whipped topping**
	Assorted Halloween candies, colored sprinkles *and* cake decorator gel, for decorating

❶ Split 15 cookies, leaving filling on 1 side of each cookie. Finely crush plain split cookies and 5 whole cookies.

❷ Mix crushed cookies, butter and sugar in small bowl. Sprinkle on bottom of 9-inch springform pan, pressing gently to form crust. Stand remaining 15 split cookies on edge around side of pan, alternating filling and cookie side out.

❸ Spread chocolate ice cream evenly on prepared crust. Coarsely chop remaining 12 cookies; stir into vanilla ice cream and spread over chocolate layer. Cover; freeze 3 hours or until firm.

❹ Remove side of pan. Pipe or spread whipped topping on top of dessert. Decorate with Halloween candies and colored sprinkles to form pumpkin patch. Using decorator gel, make pumpkin faces on the orange filling on split cookies around edge and, if desired, on additional split cookies. Stand the additional cookies on edge on top of dessert. Serve immediately. Makes 15 servings.

Halloween Cupcakes

Prep Time: 35 min.

Cast a bewitching mood at your Halloween gathering with these fun-to-make cupcakes decorated like cats and bats (photo, page 51).

- 1 **(16-ounce) can chocolate frosting, divided**
- 24 **(2½-inch) baked cupcakes**
- 12 **Halloween OREO Chocolate Sandwich Cookies**

   Black shoestring licorice, candy corn, PLANTERS COCKTAIL Peanuts, cinnamon red hots, colored sprinkles *and* assorted miniature jelly beans, for decorating

❶ Reserve ¼ cup chocolate frosting for decorating; frost the tops of cupcakes with remaining chocolate frosting.

❷ Split cookies, leaving filling on 1 side of each cookie. Decorate orange filling on split cookies to resemble cat faces using licorice for whiskers, candy corn for ears, peanuts for eyes and red hots for noses, securing with small amount of frosting.

❸ Halve plain split cookies for bat wings; decorate with colored sprinkles, securing with small amount of frosting.

❹ Stand cat faces on edge on top of 12 cupcakes; place 3-inch piece of licorice behind each cat face for tail. Arrange bat wings on top of remaining 12 cupcakes to resemble bats. Place jelly bean in center of each bat, securing with small amount of frosting. Makes 24 cupcakes.

Pumpkin Patch Cupcakes

Here's another fun Halloween cupcake idea you'll like from Oreo® Man. Split Halloween **OREO** Chocolate Sandwich Cookies, leaving the filling on one side of each cookie. Using cake decorator icing or gel, make pumpkin faces on the orange filling on split cookies. Stand the faces on edge on top of frosted cupcakes. Sprinkle green-tinted coconut on top for grass. If you like, decorate the leftover plain split cookies to resemble bats, as directed in Halloween Cupcakes (recipe, left).

OREO® Caramel-Dipped Apples

Prep Time: 20 min. plus standing • Cook Time: 10 min.

Caramel-dipped apples become gourmet delights when covered in a crunchy Oreo coating, then drizzled with white chocolate.

- **6 wooden pop sticks**
- **6 large apples, washed, well dried**
- **75 vanilla caramels (about 21 ounces), unwrapped**
- **3 tablespoons water**
- **24 Halloween OREO** *and/or* **OREO Chocolate Sandwich Cookies, coarsely chopped**
- **6 ounces white chocolate**
- **2 teaspoons vegetable oil**
- **6 sticks hard candy, optional**

❶ Insert pop stick into stem end of each apple; set aside. Heat caramels and water in large saucepan over medium-low heat, stirring until caramels are melted and smooth.

❷ Dip apples into melted caramel, spooning caramel over apples to coat. Roll in chopped cookies, pressing cookies gently into caramel. Place on waxed-paper-lined baking sheet; let stand 25 minutes or until caramel sets.

❸ Heat chocolate and oil in medium saucepan over low heat, stirring until melted and smooth; cool 15 minutes. Drizzle over apples; let stand until firm (refrigerate if needed). Store in refrigerator up to 2 days. Just before serving, replace pop sticks with hard candy, if desired. Makes 6 dipped apples.

OREO® Caramel-Dipped Apples

OREO® Mint Cocoa

Prep Time: 5 min. Cook Time: 5 min.

Here's a steamy hot beverage guests will love at your next holiday gathering. To make ahead, blend the cookie-and-milk mixture and store it in the refrigerator until you're ready to heat it.

> **10 OREO Chocolate Sandwich Cookies, coarsely chopped**
> **3 cups milk**
> **½ cup chocolate-flavored syrup**
> **½ teaspoon peppermint extract**
>   **Thawed frozen whipped topping**
> **4 candy canes *or* peppermint sticks, for garnish**

❶ Blend chopped cookies, milk, syrup and peppermint extract in electric blender until combined.

❷ Pour into 2-quart saucepan. Heat over medium-high heat, stirring frequently until hot.

❸ Ladle into 4 mugs. Top with whipped topping; garnish with candy canes. Serve warm with additional cookies, if desired. Makes 4 servings.

OREO® Mint Cocoa

OREO® Pecan Tart

Prep Time: 25 min. • Bake Time: 50 min. plus cooling

Traditional pecan pie receives a delectable makeover in this elegant cookie-laced tart. For an extra-special presentation, drizzle individual servings with fudge and caramel sauces.

	Pastry for 9-inch pie crust
26	**Holiday OREO Chocolate Sandwich Cookies, divided**
¾	**cup PLANTERS Pecans, coarsely chopped**
4	**eggs, beaten**
1	**cup sugar**
1	**cup light corn syrup**
2	**tablespoons butter *or* margarine, melted**
1	**teaspoon vanilla extract**
	Whipped cream, for garnish

❶ Roll out pastry to 12-inch circle on floured surface. Place pastry in 9-inch springform pan, pressing 1½ inches up side. Coarsely chop 20 cookies. Sprinkle chopped cookies and nuts into prepared crust; set aside.

❷ Blend eggs, sugar, corn syrup, butter and vanilla in large bowl with electric mixer at low speed; pour over cookie mixture.

❸ Bake at 400°F for 15 minutes. Reduce heat to 350°F; bake for 35 to 40 minutes or until golden brown and puffed. Cool completely in pan on wire rack.

❹ Refrigerate until serving time. Halve remaining 6 cookies; garnish tart with whipped cream and halved cookies. Makes 12 servings.

Festive Cookies

Festive Tree Cake

Prep Time: 35 min. • Bake Time: 30 min. plus cooling

With a whimsical cookie tree you create in the batter, it's never been easier to make a holiday cake.

25	**Holiday OREO Chocolate Sandwich Cookies, divided**
1	**(18.25-ounce) package white cake mix**
1¼	**cups water**
¼	**cup vegetable oil**
3	**egg whites**
1	**(4.25-ounce) tube green cake decorator icing**
	LIFE SAVERS GUMMI SAVERS Candies, candy-coated
	chocolate candies *and/or* colored sprinkles, for decorating
	Powdered sugar, for garnish

❶ Coarsely chop 15 cookies. Mix cake mix, water, oil and egg whites in large bowl with electric mixer at low speed until moistened. Beat 2 minutes at medium speed. Stir in chopped cookies. Pour into greased and floured 13x9x2-inch baking pan.

❷ Halve 8 cookies. Arrange halved cookies in rows in triangle shapes to form tree design, pressing cut side of each cookie into batter in pan (cookies will tip slightly). Press flat side of 1 whole cookie at top for star and flat side of remaining whole cookie at bottom for base.

❸ Bake at 350°F for 30 to 40 minutes or until toothpick inserted near center comes out clean. Cool in pan on wire rack 10 minutes. Remove from pan; cool completely.

❹ Place cake on serving platter. Decorate with decorator icing, candies and/or colored sprinkles. Sprinkle with powdered sugar. Cut into squares to serve. Makes 12 servings.

No time to bake holiday cookies? Don't fret. Everyone will love your decorated Oreo® cookies. To make them, simply use tubes of cake decorator icings and gels to pipe simple designs onto Fudge and White Fudge Covered OREO Chocolate Sandwich Cookies. Make snowmen, Christmas trees, Stars of David, snowflakes, holly leaves—the possibilities are endless. Or, if you like, secure small cake-top decorating candies to cookies with the icing.

OREO® White Chocolate Mousse

Prep Time: 25 min. • Chill Time: 6 hrs.

Ideal for holiday entertaining, this creamy mousse cake can be prepared up to a day in advance.

 1 **(1-pound 4-ounce) package Holiday OREO** *or*
   OREO Chocolate Sandwich Cookies, divided
 6 **tablespoons butter** *or* **margarine, melted**
 1 **envelope KNOX Unflavored Gelatine**
1¼ **cups milk**
 1 **(11-ounce) package white chocolate chips**
 1 **pint heavy cream, whipped** *or* **1 (8-ounce) container frozen**
   whipped topping, thawed
   Peppermint candies, coarsely crushed, *and* **white**
   chocolate curls (see note, page 19), for garnish

❶ Finely crush 24 cookies. Mix crushed cookies and butter in bowl. Press firmly on bottom and 1 inch up side of 9-inch springform pan. Set aside.

❷ Coarsely chop 24 cookies. Set aside. Sprinkle gelatine over cold milk in large saucepan; let stand 1 minute. Cook over low heat for 3 minutes, stirring until gelatine completely dissolves.

❸ Add white chocolate chips to gelatine mixture; continue cooking until chocolate chips are melted and smooth. Place saucepan in bowl of ice water; stirring frequently 8 to 10 minutes or until slightly thickened.

❹ Gently fold chopped cookies and whipped cream into gelatine mixture. Spoon into prepared crust. Refrigerate 6 hours or overnight. Halve remaining cookies; garnish mousse with halved cookies, peppermint candies and chocolate curls. Makes 16 servings.

OREO® White Chocolate Mousse

Bunny Cookie Pops

Prep Time: 40 min. plus standing • Cook Time: 5 min.

Bunny pops make a charming addition to anyone's Easter basket. Arrange the cookie pops upright in the grass to peek out and enchant kids and adults alike.

14 **lollipop sticks**

28 **Spring OREO Chocolate Sandwich Cookies, divided**

12 **ounces white chocolate**

1 **to 2 tablespoons vegetable oil**

**Assorted jelly beans *and* PLANTERS Slivered Almonds,
    for decorating**

❶ Insert lollipop stick into creme center of each of 14 cookies. Split the remaining 14 cookies for ears, leaving filling on 1 side of each cookie. Halve split cookies with filling; set aside (save plain split cookies for another use).

❷ Heat chocolate and 1 tablespoon oil in small saucepan over low heat, stirring until melted and smooth. Remove from heat; stir in additional oil if needed to make a pourable consistency.

❸ Dip each cookie pop into melted chocolate to coat, supporting cookie with fork to prevent cookie from detaching from stick. Place on waxed-paper-lined baking sheet.

❹ Dip points of halved cookies into melted chocolate; press 2 halved cookies against each head for ears. Decorate faces with jelly beans for eyes and noses and almonds for whiskers. Let stand until set. Makes 14 cookie pops.

Bunny
Cookie Pops

Easter Bonnet Cake

Springtime Dessert Cups

Prep Time: 30 min. • Chill Time: 1 hr.

Celebrate the arrival of spring with these colorful, decorated pudding desserts.

> 20 **Spring OREO Chocolate Sandwich Cookies, divided**
> 2 **(4-serving size) packages ROYAL Vanilla Instant Pudding & Pie Filling**
> 3 **cups milk**
> 1 **(12-ounce) container frozen whipped topping, thawed, divided**
> ½ **cup flaked coconut**
> **Green food coloring**
> **Assorted jelly beans, Easter candy corn *and* white cake**
>   **decorator icing, for decorating**

❶ Split 12 cookies, leaving filling on 1 side of each cookie. Reserve split cookies with filling for garnish. Finely crush plain split cookies and remaining 8 whole cookies; set aside.

❷ Prepare 2 packages pudding mix according to package directions using 3 cups milk. Reserve 1 cup whipped topping for garnish; fold remaining whipped topping into pudding. Stir in crushed cookies; spoon mixture into 12 (9-ounce) dessert cups. Refrigerate at least 1 hour or until serving time.

❸ Toss coconut with enough food coloring to tint green. Top dessert cups with remaining whipped topping and tinted coconut. Decorate filling on reserved split cookies with jelly beans and candy corn to resemble bunnies or sunflowers, securing with small amount of frosting. Stand decorated cookies on edge on top of dessert cups. Sprinkle with additional candies, if desired; serve immediately. Makes 12 servings.

Easter Bonnet Cake

Prep Time: 40 min. • Bake Time: 25 min. plus cooling

Welcome Easter in grand style with this dazzling bonnet cake decked out in delicious finery.

- 15 **Spring OREO Chocolate Sandwich Cookies, divided**
- 1 **(18.25-ounce) package yellow cake mix**
- 1¼ **cups water**
- ¼ **cup vegetable oil**
- 3 **eggs**
- 1 **(16-ounce) can vanilla frosting, tinted yellow, divided**
- 1 **(3.5-ounce) can flaked coconut (1⅓ cups)**
- **Colored ribbon *and* cake-top decorating flowers, for decorating**

❶ Split 11 cookies, leaving filling on 1 side of each cookie. Reserve split cookies with filling for brim of hat. Coarsely chop plain split cookies and remaining 4 whole cookies; set aside.

❷ Mix cake mix, water, oil and eggs in large bowl with electric mixer at low speed until moistened. Beat 2 minutes at medium speed. Stir in chopped cookies. Pour 3 cups batter into greased and floured 9-inch round cake pan and ¾ cup batter into greased and floured 10-ounce custard cup.

❸ Bake at 350°F for 25 to 35 minutes or until toothpick inserted near centers comes out clean. Cool in pan and custard cup on wire racks 10 minutes; remove from pan and custard cup. Cool completely. (Divide remaining batter among 6 to 8 paper-lined 2½-inch muffin pan cups. Bake at 350°F for 15 to 25 minutes. Cool in muffin pan on wire rack 5 minutes. Remove from pan, cool completely, and save cupcakes for another use.)

❹ Place 9-inch cake layer on serving plate; frost top of cake with some of the frosting. Place cake round from custard cup, top side down, slightly off-center on top of cake layer. Reserve ⅓ cup frosting for cupcakes; frost side and top of bonnet with remaining frosting. Sprinkle with coconut, pressing gently into frosting.

❺ Halve reserved split cookies. Place, filling side up and rounded edge out, around brim of hat. Place a ribbon around the center cake round to resemble a bonnet bow. Decorate with cake-top flowers. Decorate cupcakes with reserved frosting and candies. Makes 1 (9-inch) cake and 6 to 8 cupcakes.

Kids
in the
Kitchen

~

Here's a host of goodies that were tested, tasted and approved by kids ages 8 to 12. Designed for beginning cooks, each recipe includes simple-to-follow directions and, most of all, promises to be fun to make—and eat!

OREO® Pizza (recipe, page 66)

OREO® Pizza

Prep Time: 15 min. • Bake Time: 19 min.

Mama Mia—this pizza may not be Italian, but it certainly is yummy (photo, page 65).

Nonstick spray coating

30 **OREO Chocolate Sandwich Cookies,**
    divided

 1 **(19.8-ounce) package fudge**
    brownie mix

½ **cup vegetable oil**

¼ **cup water**

 2 **eggs**

1½ **cups miniature marshmallows**

¼ **cup miniature candy-coated chocolate**
   candies *or* ⅓ cup candy-coated
   chocolate candies

Utensils

12-inch pizza pan
    or 13x9x2-inch baking pan
Large plastic bag
Rolling pin
Cutting board
Sharp knife
Large bowl
Measuring cups
Wooden spoon
Rubber scraper
Hot pads
Cooling rack
Hot, wet knife

❶ Turn on oven to 350°F Spray the bottom of the pizza or baking pan with nonstick coating. Save until Step 4.

❷ Put 22 cookies in the plastic bag. Seal or tie bag closed. Use the rolling pin to *coarsely crush* the cookies. (Or, see tip, page 68.) Save until Step 3. On the cutting board, use the sharp knife to cut remaining 8 cookies into small pieces. Save until Step 7.

❸ Prepare brownie mix in the large bowl following the package directions using the oil, water and eggs. Use the scraper to stir in the crushed cookies.

❹ Pour batter into the prepared pizza or baking pan, scraping bowl with the rubber scraper to remove all the batter. Spread the batter evenly in pan. Put the pan in oven.

❺ Bake for 18 to 20 minutes for pizza pan (25 to 28 minutes for 13x9-inch pan) or until edges are firm. Use hot pads to remove the pan from oven.

❻ Sprinkle top of hot brownie with marshmallows. Use hot pads to put the pan back in oven. Bake 1 to 2 minutes more or until marshmallows are soft and puffy. Turn off oven. Use hot pads to remove the pan from oven. Set the pan on cooling rack.

❼ Sprinkle top of hot brownie with cut-up cookies and candies. Use the hot, wet knife to cut pizza into wedges or squares. Serve warm. Makes 12 servings.

OREO® Milk Shake

Prep Time: 15 min.

How long have milk shakes been around? Longer than you might guess. The first milk shakes were invented right here in America almost 100 years ago.

> 1 **pint vanilla ice cream**
> 15 **OREO Chocolate Sandwich Cookies, divided**
> ½ **cup milk**
> ¼ **cup chocolate-flavored syrup**
> **Banana slices *and* fresh strawberries, for garnish**

❶ Soften ice cream by letting it stand at room temperature for 10 to 15 minutes. Put 14 cookies in the plastic bag. Seal or tie bag closed. Use the rolling pin to *coarsely crush* the cookies. (Or, see tip, page 68.) Save until Step 2. Use your hands to break the remaining 1 cookie into quarters; save until Step 3.

❷ Put ice cream, crushed cookies, milk and chocolate syrup in the blender. Blend until smooth, stopping blender 4 or 5 times to push down mixture with the rubber scraper.

❸ Pour the mixture into glasses. Put banana, strawberries and reserved quartered cookie on skewers; put skewers in glasses. Serve immediately. Makes 4 servings.

Utensils
Large plastic bag
Rolling pin
Ice cream scoop
Measuring cups
Electric blender
Rubber scraper
4 (8-ounce) glasses
4 short wooden skewers

OREO® Milk Shake

Crushing Oreo Cookies

Hey, kids! Are you having trouble using a rolling pin to crush the Oreo cookies? If so, here are some other methods that may be easier for you.

• Seal the cookies in a large plastic bag. Then use your hands or the flat side of a meat mallet to coarsely or finely crush the cookies.

• With adult help, put the cookies in a blender container. Cover and blend to finely crush the cookies.

OREO® Banana Peanut Butter Treats

Prep Time: 15 min. • Freeze Time: 2 hrs.

This peanutty coating is also good on apples. Simply spread some peanut butter onto apple wedges; then roll them in the cookie mixture.

- 12 **OREO Chocolate Sandwich Cookies**
- 2 **tablespoons colored sprinkles**
- 4 **firm ripe bananas**
- ¾ **cup creamy peanut butter**

Utensils		
Large plastic bag	Pie plate	8 wooden pop sticks
Rolling pin	Spoon	Plastic wrap
Measuring cups *and* spoons	Table knife	

❶ Put cookies in the plastic bag. Seal or tie bag closed. Use the rolling pin to *finely crush* the cookies. (Or, see tip, left.)

❷ Put crushed cookies and colored sprinkles in the pie plate. Stir together with the spoon.

❸ Use the table knife to cut each banana in half crosswise. Slide a pop stick into cut end of each banana.

❹ Use the table knife to spread each banana with peanut butter. Roll each banana in cookie mixture to coat.

❺ Wrap each coated banana in plastic wrap and freeze 2 hours or until firm. Makes 8 servings.

Snack-Attack Mix

Prep Time: 10 min.

When hunger pangs attack, satisfy them with this easy-to-make snack mix.

16 **OREO** *or* **OREO DOUBLE STUF Chocolate Sandwich Cookies**

1 **(7-ounce) package LIFE SAVERS GUMMI SAVERS Wild Berry Candies**

1 **cup Teddy Grahams DIZZY GRIZZLIES Frosted Grahams**

1 **(5-ounce) package SNACKWELL'S Raisin Dips Candy**

1 **cup PLANTERS Mini Pretzel Twists, coarsely broken**

Utensils
Large plastic bag
Measuring cups
Large airtight container

❶ Put cookies in the plastic bag. Seal or tie bag closed. Use your hands to break the cookies into large pieces.

❷ Open bag and add berry candies, grahams, raisin candy and pretzels. Seal or tie bag closed; shake to combine.

❸ Store in airtight container or plastic bag. Makes 6 cups.

Safety Smarts

When in the kitchen, remind kids of these important tips:

- **Before starting to cook, ask them to roll up their sleeves, tie back their hair if it is long and put on a clean apron.**
- **Wash hands well with soap and water.**
- **Be sure they read the recipe and gather all of the ingredients and utensils that they'll need.**
- **Have them ask an adult to help them whenever they use the oven, stove top, microwave oven, electric blender or a sharp knife, or if they need to lift something heavy like a large saucepan.**
- **Remind them to use hot pads to handle anything that is warm or hot.**

OREO® Cereal Bars

Prep Time: 10 min. plus standing • Cook Time: 10 min.

Like magic, you can change these bars by simply switching the cereal. It's fun to mix two or three different cereals together. Just be sure to use only 4 cups total.

> **Nonstick spray coating**
> **32 OREO Chocolate Sandwich Cookies**
> **4 cups round toasted whole-grain oat cereal**
> **⅓ cup butter or margarine**
> **1 (10½-ounce) package miniature marshmallows**

❶ Spray the bottom of the pan with nonstick coating. Spray the rubber scraper with nonstick coating. Save until Step 4.

❷ Put cookies in the plastic bag. Seal or tie bag closed. Use the rolling pin to *coarsely crush* the cookies. (Or, see tip, page 68.) Put crushed cookies and cereal in the bowl. Stir together with the wooden spoon.

❸ Put butter and marshmallows in the saucepan. Put on burner and turn to medium-low heat. Cook until butter and marshmallows are melted and smooth, stirring all the time with the wooden spoon. Turn off burner. Remove pan from burner. Pour the marshmallow mixture over cookie mixture. Quickly stir together with the wooden spoon until ingredients are evenly coated.

❹ Use the prepared rubber scraper to push the mixture into the prepared pan. Press evenly in pan. Let stand at room temperature until set. Use the table knife to cut cereal bars into squares. Store in airtight container. Makes 24 bars.

Utensils
13x9x2-inch pan
Rubber scraper
Large plastic bag
Rolling pin
Measuring cups
Large bowl
Wooden spoon
Large saucepan
Table knife

OREO® Ice Cream

OREO® Ice Cream

Prep Time: 15 min. • Freeze Time: 2 hrs.

For fun with friends, have an ice cream party. Make this Oreo-accented treat with different flavors of ice cream; then let everyone sample your rainbow of creations.

1 quart ice cream, any flavor

20 OREO *or* OREO DOUBLE STUF Chocolate Sandwich Cookies

Gumdrops, for garnish

Utensils
Large plastic bag
Rolling pin
Spoon
Measuring cups
Large bowl
Rubber scraper
Large plastic container

❶ Soften ice cream by letting it stand at room temperature for 10 to 15 minutes. Put cookies in the plastic bag. Seal or tie bag closed. Use the rolling pin to *coarsely crush* the cookies. (Or, see tip, page 68.)

❷ Put the softened ice cream and crushed cookies in the bowl. Stir together with the rubber scraper.

❸ Use the rubber scraper to push the mixture into the plastic container. Cover and freeze 2 hours or until firm. Garnish each serving with gumdrops and, if desired, additional cookies. Makes 6 to 8 servings.

Rocky Mallow Road Ice Cream: Prepare OREO® Ice Cream as directed, except stir 1 cup miniature marshmallows into the ice cream mixture in step 2.

Peanutty Ice Cream: Prepare OREO® Ice Cream as directed, except stir ½ cup PLANTERS COCKTAIL Peanuts into the ice cream mixture in step 2.

Triple-Chip Topping

Keep this fun and easy topping on hand to spoon over ice cream, cut-up fruit or pudding.

Put 10 OREO *or* OREO DOUBLE STUF Chocolate Sandwich Cookies in a large plastic bag. Seal or tie bag closed. Use your hands to break the cookies into large pieces. Put broken cookies, ½ cup miniature semisweet chocolate chips, ½ cup white chocolate chips and ½ cup peanut butter chips in a medium bowl. Stir together with a spoon. Store in an airtight container for up to 2 weeks. Makes 2½ cups.

OREO® Speckled Cream

Prep Time: 5 min. • Chill Time: 2 hrs.

If you like, add a splash of color to the whipped topping by gently stirring in a few drops of food coloring before mixing it with the Oreo cookies.

16 OREO *or* OREO DOUBLE STUF Chocolate Sandwich Cookies

2 cups thawed frozen whipped topping

❶ Put cookies in the plastic bag. Seal or tie bag closed. Use the rolling pin to *coarsely crush* the cookies. (Or, see tip, page 68.)

❷ Put crushed cookies and whipped topping in the bowl. Gently stir together with the rubber scraper. Cover and refrigerate at least 2 hours or up to 24 hours.

❸ Serve as a topping for cake, brownies or cut-up fruit. Makes about 10 servings (2½ cups).

Utensils
Large plastic bag
Rolling pin
Measuring cups
Medium bowl
Rubber scraper

Awesome Sites

Hey, kids! Join Oreo Man to check out the Oreo and Nabisco web sites.

Peanut Butter S'Mores

Prep Time: 20 min. • Microwave Time: 20 sec.

The addition of peanut butter and Oreo® cookies turns regular s'mores into extraordinary treats.

- **4 OREO Chocolate Sandwich Cookies**
- **3 tablespoons creamy peanut butter**
- **8 squares HONEY MAID Honey Grahams**
- **I tablespoon hot fudge sauce**
- **¼ cup miniature marshmallows**

❶ Put cookies in the plastic bag. Seal or tie bag closed. Use your hands to break the cookies into large pieces. Save until Step 3.

❷ Use table knife to spread I teaspoon peanut butter on I side of each graham square.

❸ Using 4 graham squares, top the peanut butter side of each square with I tablespoon broken cookies, ¾ teaspoon fudge sauce and 4 or 5 miniature marshmallows. Top with remaining 4 graham squares, peanut butter side down, pressing gently to form sandwiches.

❹ Place on the microwavable plate. Microwave on HIGH (100% power) for 20 to 30 seconds or until heated through. Serve warm. Makes 4 servings.

Utensils
Large plastic bag
Table knife
Measuring cups *and* spoons
Microwavable plate

For Oreo fun and games, visit **www.oreo.com.** Here you'll find lots of Oreo trivia, recipes and activities. Next, log on to **www.nabisco.com** to travel through the Nabisco Neighborhood. You'll learn about the entire family of Nabisco products along with finding more recipes and cool games to play.

OREO® Dirt Cups

OREO® Dirt Cups

Prep Time: 20 min. • Chill Time: 1 hr.

It's hard to tell what's more fun—making these dessert cups or eating them!

20 OREO Chocolate Sandwich Cookies

1 (4-serving size) package ROYAL Vanilla Instant Pudding & Pie Filling

4 cups milk, divided

1 cup thawed frozen whipped topping, divided

1 (4-serving size) package ROYAL Chocolate Instant Pudding & Pie Filling

16 gummy worms, for garnish

Utensils		
Large plastic bag	**Measuring cups**	**2 rubber scrapers**
Rolling pin	***and* spoons**	**8 (6-ounce) dessert cups**
2 medium bowls	**2 wire whisks**	
	***or* a rotary beater**	

❶ Put cookies in the plastic bag. Seal or tie bag closed. Use the rolling pin to *finely crush* the cookies. (Or, see tip, page 68.) Save until Step 4.

❷ Put vanilla pudding mix in one of the bowls. Add 2 cups milk to pudding. Use a wire whisk or the rotary beater to beat until well mixed. Let stand 5 minutes. Use a rubber scraper to gently stir in ½ cup whipped topping. Set aside. Wash rotary beater, if using.

❸ Put chocolate pudding mix in the other bowl. Add remaining 2 cups milk to pudding. Use the other wire whisk or the rotary beater to beat until well mixed. Let stand 5 minutes. Use the other rubber scraper to gently stir in the remaining ½ cup whipped topping.

❹ Sprinkle 1 tablespoon crushed cookies into bottom of each dessert cup. Top each with ¼ cup vanilla pudding, 1 tablespoon crushed cookies and ¼ cup chocolate pudding. Top with remaining crushed cookies.

❺ Refrigerate at least 1 hour. Before serving, put 2 gummy worms on top of each serving. Makes 8 servings.

Conehead Parfaits

Prep Time: 10 min. • Freeze Time: 1 hr.

These funny upside-down ice cream cones are a blast to decorate. Make your conehead's face as silly as you can.

1	**quart ice cream, any flavor**
8	**OREO Chocolate Cones**
24	**OREO Chocolate Sandwich Cookies**
	LIFE SAVERS GUMMI SAVERS Candies, PLANTERS COCKTAIL Peanuts, BUBBLE YUM Cotton Candy Bubble Gum, fruit roll-ups *and/or* other assorted small candies, for decorating

Utensils	
Baking sheet	**Medium ice cream scoop**
Waxed paper	**8 dessert plates**

❶ Line the baking sheet with waxed paper.

❷ Using the ice cream scoop, scoop ice cream into 8 balls and put on prepared baking sheet. Put a chocolate cone on top of each ice cream ball for a hat. Freeze 1 hour or until firm.

❸ Put 3 cookies in a circle on each plate. Put frozen ice cream scoops on top of cookies. Decorate faces with candies and nuts. Makes 8 servings.

Oreo Math

Mom and Dad—playing with numbers can be a real treat, especially when it's done with Oreo® cookies.

To do so, take the "lid" off at least 13 OREO DOUBLE STUF Chocolate Sandwich Cookies. Using cake decorator gels, write numbers 0 through 9 and "minus," "plus" and "equals" signs on the filling side of each split cookie (use the plain split cookies as prizes while playing the game).

To play the game, have your child arrange the cookies in numerical order. Or, create arithmetic problems for your child to solve.

Peanut Butter Chocolate Bites

Prep Time: 30 min. • Freeze Time: 30 min. • Chill Time: 30 min.

Surprise a special friend or your mom or dad with a box of homemade candies—made by you!

36 OREO Chocolate Sandwich Cookies, divided

½ cup creamy peanut butter

1⅓ cups semisweet chocolate chips

❶ Line the baking sheet with waxed paper. Save until Step 4.

❷ Put 16 cookies in one of the plastic bags. Seal or tie bag closed. Use the rolling pin to *finely crush* the cookies. (Or, see tip, page 68.) Save until Step 6.

❸ Put remaining 20 cookies in the other plastic bag. Seal or tie bag closed. Use the rolling pin to *finely crush* the cookies. Put crushed cookies and peanut butter in the large bowl. Stir together with the wooden spoon. Cover and freeze 20 minutes or until firm enough to handle.

❹ Pinch off small pieces of peanut butter mixture and firmly press each piece between your fingers to form a 1-inch ball. Place on the prepared baking sheet and freeze 10 minutes or until firm.

❺ Meanwhile, put chocolate chips in the microwavable bowl. Microwave on HIGH (100% power) for 1½ to 2½ minutes or until the chocolate is soft enough to stir smooth, stirring once every minute with the wooden spoon. Use the hot pads to remove bowl from microwave oven.

❻ Dip each frozen ball in the melted chocolate to coat. Remove with the fork, letting extra chocolate drip off. Roll each ball in the reserved crushed cookies. Put on the prepared baking sheet and refrigerate 30 minutes or until firm. Store in airtight container in refrigerator. Makes 2 dozen.

Utensils
Baking sheet
Waxed paper
2 large plastic bags
Rolling pin
Measuring cups
Large bowl
Wooden spoon
Small microwavable bowl
Hot pads
Fork
Airtight container

Cookie *Crafts*

Both young and old will enjoy making these delightful food crafts. A towering rocket ship, an adorable smiling inchworm and a pot of whimsical flowers are just a few of the many cookie creations you'll find on the following pages.

Train Engine (directions, page 94)

Ladybug

1 OREO DOUBLE STUF Chocolate Sandwich Cookie

1 to 2 teaspoons canned vanilla frosting, tinted red

10 miniature semisweet chocolate chips

1 small red *or* black gumdrop

Black shoestring licorice

❶ Split cookie, leaving filling on 1 side of cookie. Halve split cookie with filling for wings; spread plain sides with red frosting. Press chocolate chips into red frosting on wings for spots.

❷ Secure wings, frosted sides up and rounded edges out, with frosting to top of plain split cookie, separating wings slightly.

❸ Halve gumdrop horizontally; press cut ends together for head. Cut licorice into 2 (2-inch) pieces for antennae. Make 2 holes in head with toothpick; push antennae into holes. Secure head with frosting to body. Makes 1 ladybug.

Ladybug

Butterfly

Butterfly

2 OREO DOUBLE STUF Chocolate Sandwich Cookies, divided

2 tablespoons canned vanilla frosting, tinted yellow

3 small green gumdrops, divided

Red shoestring licorice

2 LIFE SAVERS GUMMI SAVERS Candies, halved

Miniature candy-coated chocolate candies

❶ Split 1 cookie through filling; halve each side for wings. Spread plain sides of wings with yellow frosting. Spread remaining whole cookie with frosting for base. Press wings, frosted side up and rounded edge out, onto base.

❷ Trim a thin slice off wide ends of 2 gumdrops; press cut ends together for body. Trim a thin slice off body and another thin slice off narrow end of remaining gumdrop for head; reserve slices for decorating, if desired. Press head to body.

❸ Cut licorice into 2 (2-inch) pieces for antennae. Make 2 holes in head with toothpick; push antennae into holes. Secure body on top of wings with frosting. Decorate wings with thin gumdrop slices (if desired), gummi candies and miniature candies. Makes 1 butterfly.

OREO® Man

1 OREO DOUBLE STUF Chocolate Sandwich Cookie
   White cake decorator icing
2 blue *and* 1 red miniature candy-coated chocolate candies
2 miniature semisweet chocolate chips
   Red shoestring licorice
2 pieces BUBBLE YUM Cotton Candy Gum
1 white chenille stem

❶ Using cookie for face, pipe icing in 2 ovals for whites of eyes. Press blue candies into icing for irises of eyes; secure chocolate chips to blue candies with icing for pupils. Press 2 small pieces of licorice into icing above eyes for eyebrows.

❷ Pipe icing onto cookie for mouth. Halve red candy; secure 1 half to cookie with icing for nose (save remaining half for another use). Pipe icing on top for hair.

❸ For feet and hands, halve gum pieces. Roll 2 halves into ovals for feet. Split 1 half (save remaining half for another use); roll into 2 balls and flatten and shape for hands.

❹ For legs and arms, cut chenille stem into 2 (2-inch) and 2 (1-inch) pieces. Insert 2-inch pieces into feet; insert 1-inch pieces into hands. Insert legs and arms into cookie. Makes 1 Oreo character.

Oreo Stack-Scrapers

The next time your children say there's nothing to do, put their hands and imaginations to play by making Oreo towers that reach for the sky. Give them packages of Oreo cookies for the building blocks and canned frosting for mortar. Provide other sweets, such as Oreo cones and Comet cups for tower toppers, Honey Maid grahams for floors and skywalks and small candies for architectural trims.

It's OREO® Time!

½   **cup light corn syrup**

¼   **cup packed brown sugar**

I   **cup creamy peanut butter**

30   **OREO Chocolate Sandwich Cookies, divided**

2   **cups crisp rice cereal**

¾   **cup canned vanilla frosting, tinted orange**
     Red, purple *and/or* green cake decorator gels

2   **LIFE SAVERS GUMMI SAVERS Candies**

2   **sticks FRUIT STRIPE Bubble Gum**

❶ Heat corn syrup and brown sugar in medium saucepan to a boil. Stir in peanut butter; remove from heat.

❷ Coarsely chop 18 cookies. Stir chopped cookies and cereal into peanut butter mixture. Press firmly into greased and waxed-paper-lined 9-inch round cake pan. Refrigerate I hour or until firm.

❸ Invert onto serving plate; remove waxed paper. Spread frosting over top of cereal mixture. Split remaining 12 cookies, leaving filling on I side of each cookie. Using gels, write numbers I through 12 on filling side of each split cookie (save plain split cookies for another use); press around edge for numbers of clock.

❹ Press gummi candies into center of clock. Cut sticks of gum to form minute and hour hands; press onto clock. Makes 8 servings.

OREO® Rocket Ship

13 OREO DOUBLE STUF Chocolate Sandwich Cookies

¼ **cup canned vanilla frosting**

Blue food coloring

1 OREO Chocolate Cone

Cinnamon red hots

Red cake decorator gel, for decorating

4 sticks FRUIT STRIPE Bubble Gum

❶ Stack cookies together, securing with some frosting in between each cookie. Let dry completely.

❷ Tint remaining frosting with food coloring; spread cone with blue frosting. Press red hots into frosting around open end of cone. Let dry. Write USA on cone with gel.

❸ Trim ends of gum diagonally; secure with gel around base of rocket. Secure cone with frosting to top of rocket. Decorate rocket with red hots. Makes 1 rocket ship.

Note: If you like, surround rocket ship with mounds of pressurized whipped topping for clouds and red candy curls for blast-off trails. To make red candy curls, pipe a small amount of melted red candy coating in spiral shapes onto waxed paper; refrigerate until set. Carefully peel off paper.

OREO® Rocket Ship

Blooming OREO® Cookies

4 **wooden pop sticks**

4 **OREO DOUBLE STUF Chocolate Sandwich Cookies**

2 **ounces vanilla-flavored candy coating, coarsely chopped**

Assorted jelly beans, gumdrops, LIFE SAVERS
   GUMMI SAVERS Candies, miniature semisweet
   chocolate chips, miniature candy-coated chocolate
   candies *and/or* colored sprinkles, for decorating

Canned vanilla frosting, optional

❶ Insert wooden stick about halfway into filling of each cookie.

❷ Heat coating in small saucepan over low heat, stirring until melted and smooth. Remove from heat.

Blooming OREO® Cookies

Spoon coating over front and side of each cookie to coat lightly (do not coat the back). Place on waxed-paper-lined baking sheet. Let stand 10 minutes or until coating starts to set.

Decorate with candies and/or sprinkles. If coating becomes too firm, secure candies with frosting. Place in refrigerator for 5 minutes or until coating hardens completely. Makes cookie flowers.

Note: If you like, present flowers in pots. Set 4 COMET RAINBOW Cups in a baking pan; spoon about 3 tablespoons any flavor cake batter into each cup. Bake at 350°F for 20 to 25 minutes or until toothpick inserted near centers comes out clean.

Cool in pan 3 minutes. Remove from pan; cool completely. Frost tops of cakes. Insert 1 or 2 flowers into each pot. Toss shredded coconut with enough green food coloring to tint green; sprinkle on top of frosting.

Cookie Critters

Cookie Critters

**5 OREO Chocolate Sandwich
     Cookies, divided**

¼ cup canned chocolate *or* vanilla frosting

Miniature marshmallows

**Miniature candy-coated chocolate candies *and/or* miniature semisweet
    chocolate chips and white cake decorator icing, for decorating**

Fruit roll-up

Red *or* black shoestring licorice

❶ Stack 4 cookies together, securing with frosting in between each cookie for body; set on edge. Secure remaining 1 cookie with frosting to 1 end, slightly higher than other cookies, for head. Let dry 15 minutes.

❷ Secure 4 marshmallows or 2 marshmallows plus 1 additional halved cookie with frosting on each side of body for paws.

❸ Decorate face with candies, icing and, if desired, additional marshmallows. Cut fruit roll-up for ears and licorice for whiskers and tail (use toothpick to make hole in cookie filling to attach tail); secure with icing. Makes 1 critter.

OREO® Inchworm

10 OREO Chocolate Sandwich Cookies, divided

¼ cup canned chocolate *or* vanilla frosting

Cake decorator icing *and/or* gel, for decorating

Shredded coconut

Green food coloring

6 LIFE SAVERS GUMMI SAVERS Candies, halved

❶ Stack 9 cookies together, securing with frosting in between each cookie for body; set on edge.

❷ Using remaining cookie for face, decorate with icing and/or gel. Secure face with frosting to 1 end of body, slightly higher than other cookies. Let dry 15 minutes.

❸ Toss coconut with enough food coloring to tint green. Frost base of inchworm with frosting; dip in tinted coconut. Secure gummi candies with frosting on each side of body for legs. Makes 1 inchworm.

OREO® Inchworm

There's No Place Like This Home

Clear packing tape

1 **(½-gallon) empty milk *or* orange juice carton**

11 **whole HONEY MAID Honey Grahams**

1 **(16-ounce) can vanilla frosting**

11 **OREO DOUBLE STUF Chocolate Sandwich Cookies**

5 **sticks hard candy, divided**

1 **TOASTETTES Frosted Strawberry Toaster Pastry**

White cake decorator icing

3 **sticks FRUIT STRIPE Bubble Gum**

1 **COMET Cup**

LIFE SAVERS GUMMI SAVERS Candies *and* assorted small gumdrops, for decorating

❶ Tape top of carton closed. Cut off and discard bottom 3½ inches so sides measure 4 inches high. Secure grahams with frosting to carton, cutting to fit as needed. Let dry.

❷ Split cookies; remove filling to make 22 chocolate wafers (save 1 wafer for another use). Halve 5 wafers. For each side of roof, use 8 whole wafers and 5 halved wafers for shingles. Secure wafers with frosting to roof, starting with bottom row and working upward. Secure 1 stick of candy to top with frosting.

❸ Score, then break remaining hard candy into 4-inch sticks; secure with frosting to corners of house. Cut toaster pastry to fit for door; secure with frosting to front. Draw windows with icing on back and sides. Halve sticks of gum crosswise for shutters; secure with frosting next to windows.

❹ Cut ice cream cup diagonally with scissors; secure with frosting to roof for chimney. Finish decorating with icing, gummi candies, gumdrops and, if desired, additional cookies. Makes 1 house.

Note: If you like, use additional cookies for path and fence, coconut for snow, hard candy and gumdrops for light pole and OREO Chocolate Cones sprinkled with powdered sugar for trees.

Train Engine

All aboard! This sweet replica of an old-time train engine makes a delightful birthday-cake topper for a young child. Fill the engine compartment with an OREO® Man, small toys or additional candy (photo, page 81).

8 whole HONEY MAID Honey Grahams, divided

⅓ to ½ cup canned vanilla frosting

8 OREO Chocolate Sandwich Cookies, divided

7 LIFE SAVERS GUMMI SAVERS Candies

1 OREO Chocolate Cone

7 assorted small gumdrops

3 sticks FRUIT STRIPE Bubble Gum

❶ Stack 5 grahams together, securing with frosting in between each for base.

❷ Break 2 grahams in half, making 4 squares. Set aside 1 square for the back of engine compartment. Break second square in half; set aside 1 piece for front (save remaining piece for another use). Cut windows in upper right and upper left corners of remaining 2 squares for sides.

❸ Cut remaining graham 3½ inches long for top. Assemble the compartment and secure with frosting to base.

❹ Cut one-quarter off 4 cookies. Stack cookies side by side, securing with frosting in between each cookie for engine; secure with frosting to base. Secure remaining 4 cookies and 2 gummi candies with frosting to base for wheels.

❺ For smokestack, score around cone 2¼ inches from tip, then cut through. Trim a thin slice off both ends of 1 gumdrop. Make a hole in gumdrop with toothpick; press tip of cone into hole. Secure with frosting to 1 gummi candy, then to engine.

❻ Secure remaining 4 gummi candies with frosting to cookie wheels. Trim thin slices off remaining 6 gumdrops (save slices for another use); press gumdrops onto wheels and engine. For cowcatcher, cut sticks of gum as shown in pattern below; secure with frosting to base. Makes 1 train engine.

Note: If you like, use red licorice to make train track. For stop sign, write on small flat lollipop with cake decorator icing.

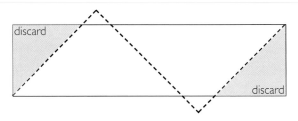

Index

Metric Cooking Hints

By making a few conversions, cooks in Australia, Canada and the United Kingdom can use these recipes with confidence. The charts on this page provide a guide for converting measurements from the U.S. customary system, which is used throughout this book, to the imperial and metric systems. There also is a conversion table for oven temperatures to accommodate the differences in oven calibrations.

Product Differences: Most of the ingredients called for in the recipes in this book are available in English-speaking countries. However, some are known by different names. Here are some common American ingredients and their possible counterparts:
- Sugar is granulated or castor sugar.
- Powdered sugar is icing sugar.
- All-purpose flour is plain household flour or white flour. When self-rising flour is used in place of all-purpose flour in a recipe that calls for leavening, omit the leavening agent (baking soda or baking powder) and salt.
- Light-colored corn syrup is golden syrup.
- Cornstarch is cornflour.
- Baking soda is bicarbonate of soda.
- Vanilla is vanilla essence.
- Green, red, or yellow bell peppers are capsicums.
- Golden raisins are sultanas.

Volume and Weight: Americans traditionally use cup measures for liquid and solid ingredients. The chart, above right, shows the approximate imperial and metric equivalents. If you are accustomed to weighing solid ingredients, the following approximate equivalents will be helpful.
- 1 cup butter, castor sugar or rice = 8 ounces = about 250 grams
- 1 cup flour = 4 ounces = about 125 grams
- 1 cup icing sugar = 5 ounces = about 150 grams

Spoon measures are used for smaller amounts of ingredients. Although the size of the tablespoon varies slightly in different countries, for practical purposes and for recipes in this book, a straight substitution is all that's necessary.

Measurements made using cups or spoons always should be level unless stated otherwise.

Equivalents: U.S. = Australia/U.K.

$\frac{1}{8}$ teaspoon = 0.5 ml
$\frac{1}{4}$ teaspoon = 1 ml
$\frac{1}{2}$ teaspoon = 2 ml
1 teaspoon = 5 ml
1 tablespoon = 1 tablespoon
$\frac{1}{4}$ cup = 2 tablespoons = 2 fluid ounces = 60 ml
$\frac{1}{3}$ cup = $\frac{1}{4}$ cup = 3 fluid ounces = 90 ml
$\frac{1}{2}$ cup = $\frac{1}{3}$ cup = 4 fluid ounces = 120 ml
$\frac{2}{3}$ cup = $\frac{1}{2}$ cup = 5 fluid ounces = 150 ml
$\frac{3}{4}$ cup = $\frac{2}{3}$ cup = 6 fluid ounces = 180 ml
1 cup = $\frac{3}{4}$ cup = 8 fluid ounces = 240 ml
$1\frac{1}{4}$ cups = 1 cup
2 cups = 1 pint
1 quart = 1 liter
$\frac{1}{2}$ inch = 1.27 cm
1 inch = 2.54 cm

Baking Pan Sizes

American	Metric
8×1½-inch round baking pan	20×4-cm cake tin
9×1½-inch round baking pan	23×3.5-cm cake tin
11×7×1½-inch baking pan	28×18×4-cm baking tin
13×9×2-inch baking pan	30×20×3-cm baking tin
2-quart rectangular baking dish	30×20×3-cm baking tin
15×10×1-inch baking pan	30×25×2-cm baking tin (Swiss roll tin)
9-inch pie plate	22×4- or 23×4-cm pie plate
7- or 8-inch springform pan	18- or 20-cm springform or loose-bottom cake tin
9×5×3-inch loaf pan	23×13×7-cm or 2-pound narrow loaf tin or pâté tin
1½-quart casserole	1.5-liter casserole
2-quart casserole	2-liter casserole

Oven Temperature Equivalents

Fahrenheit Setting	Celsius Setting*	Gas Setting
300°F	150°C	Gas Mark 2 (slow)
325°F	160°C	Gas Mark 3 (moderately slow)
350°F	180°C	Gas Mark 4 (moderate)
375°F	190°C	Gas Mark 5 (moderately hot)
400°F	200°C	Gas Mark 6 (hot)
425°F	220°C	Gas Mark 7
450°F	230°C	Gas Mark 8 (very hot)
Broil		Grill

*Electric and gas ovens may be calibrated using Celsius. However, for an electric oven, increase the Celsius setting 10 to 20 degrees when cooking above 160°C. For convection or forced-air ovens (gas or electric), lower the temperature setting 10°C when cooking at all heat levels.